DIRTY LOOKS

Cheryl Follon was born in Ayrshire, where she grew up. She studied Law and then English and Scottish Literature at Glasgow University before taking an MPhil in Creative Writing at Trinity College Dublin, and now teaches at a college of further education in Glasgow. She has received two writer's bursaries from the Scottish Arts Council, and has published two collections with Bloodaxe, *All Your Talk* (2004) and *Dirty Looks* (2010).

CHERYL FOLLON
DIRTY LOOKS

BLOODAXE BOOKS

ISBN: 978 1 85224 865 9

First published 2010 by
Bloodaxe Books Ltd,
Highgreen,
Tarset,
Northumberland NE48 1RP.

www.bloodaxebooks.com
For further information about Bloodaxe titles
please visit our website or write to
the above address for a catalogue.

Supported by
**ARTS COUNCIL
ENGLAND**

ACKNOWLEDGEMENTS
Some of these poems were first published in *Gutter*
and *Slashstroke*. And a big thanks to Sandy Hutchinson.

Cover design: Neil Astley & Pamela Robertson-Pearce

Printed in Great Britain by
Bell & Bain Limited, Glasgow, Scotland.

CONTENTS

❦

A Love Potion Concocted Together with Leaves

Careful, careful – as mother's recipe said –
add in the something leaves,
one at a time is best;

snip-snip the Seven Sisters' rose
like it was the littlest toe
of your lover in bed.

Mule Henry in Jackson Square

Let me tell you a story about my mother;
half her head rotted away
when a neurosis held sway;

it ate through her head
like a cheese.
I watched her in the bed and said goodbye.

Father ran away when I was seven –
disappearing with a fair
dressed in a costume

like an old-style harlequin,
but with roses in his hair
and two wicker baskets of yellowy plums.

I ride a cart to Jackson Square for market
and midday auction
every second Saturday.

I've a mule called Henry
and he's got no tongue.
A man from Bogalusa does my accounts.

And we have many lovely things for sale:
just you wait and see;
have a look around

and see what you can find,
there's no requirement to buy.
Do you like this ribbon in old Henry's tail?

Here's a supper bell and rare cloudy glass.
Here's an assortment of fans
with long dyed ostrich feathers;

antique furniture,
fine old chinaware
and a tiny blackberry-coloured carriage.

There're lovely things to see; a birdy cage
made for love birds;
a violet-coloured rug

and a Chinese beetle –
hold out your hand.
Here's a dice table and a hangman's watch.

A chair that belonged to the Sun King himself.
Here're bronzes and busts
and a little egg-timer,

books and pictures.
Here's a jelly mould
and a pair of pistols – hold out your hand!

Homecoming

O tippy-toe – heh, heh – and here we go –
    hush now, pussy willow man,
    honey bear, my sweet!
    Tiptoe now, so quiet –
hear – don't wake that ancient bulldog Clint.

She'll be – heh, heh – in that old bed now –
    I'm going to get in there,
    right up close, say Fuck You –
    I'll say Fuuuuuck *You!*
like an ear trumpet, very loud and clear.

Voyage In

Oh aye, here's the soft winds; the fifty-five
species of rock dove; the red fringed
dwarf mushroom; the majestic stork; the scalp.

The ten toes of wisdom; the nail varnish
taken up and applied just so; the old corals;
the pink brandies of the lips; the lappy gullies;

the fronded inlets; the bays where salt tigers go;
the soft winds; the calves and the shins
curved like a moon; the wicked cross currents;

the tug of the shallows; raccoons and their germs;
the soft winds travelling part way there and back;
the lips; the teeth; the filthy dirty fancy looks.

O Wildwood Bouquet!

I'm going to round off this head of kale.
My trusty putty-knife can clip
nice, and clip again

till it resembles the big limes
that ache and dilly-dance
and lollop round the pick-up truck.

I'm going to round off this head of kale
and pack it sweet beside
the yellow slips that are my butter-breaths.

I can tie it all up sweet and neat
with a piece of soft wire
taken from the hood of Johnstone's big car.

And here I'll fasten on the dancing beads
that laced in old Medusa's hair
when she rode the speckled horse

into a Baptist town called Bunkie
and broke open a watermelon
with a little Bowie knife kept by her hip.

I'm going to slice and nip this curly kale
till it's good for giving you.
Nice as when Lacy ran the length

of old Godiva Street
with her face bright red
because Archibald's sister had swallowed a nail.

I'll place it in a big posy of butter-breaths
like an ounce of gold.
Miss Shirley keeps these in a jar

by her grandson's door
and she can smell them at midnight,
even when it's cold. I'm going to pare this kale.

Honey

According to Nemesis' erotic handbook
　　The Night and the Perfumed Rose –
written in a dripping cave
sometime in the fifteenth century
somewhere in the foothills of old Greece –
a buttered bowl of honey's what you need
mixed with chicken stock to make a soup.
　　The thing for the lover of all lovers –
to pluck the thick gold honey
from the thick of the locust tree
with a long thin barb
and your five fingers spread out for balance.

Old Rice Road Is Crazy

Here's the short bed with its creamy lace –
thin and fine as spider webs,
of course, and weaved by ladies

with their nimble black fingers
and silver-tipped needles
in a small room in a town called Hills.

More lovely that the lovers' ancient tree
where they kiss and canoodle
and take their ugly dogs to walk

or that nook in the Café D'Or
where lovers like to take their cake and tea;
I take my lovers up the Old Rice Road.

Here's a mouthful of Indian black pearls
and salvia for a bath;
a scrap of lace, a dead man's foot,

soiled panties and iron nails.
Nothing works better than love charms
tucked up in a pouch over puttering flames.

The perfumed bed – aloes,
cinnamon and cloves
and a good dose from a pot of myrrh.

No matter that crazy papa used this bed
when he finally lost his head
and flew out the window!

The soft black figs and the prickled pears,
the honey-soaked apples;
as we passed from one mouth to another

the juices turned to brandies
in their golden jars.
The lotus blossoms melt against my thighs!

I'll press a poison leaf inside my locket
and lose it in your tea!
I take my lovers up the Old Rice Road.

Terrible Bread

Have you ever heard of 'terrible bread'?
    They've had it in London
    for over four centuries.
  I've even tried it out myself.
It's the sweetest thing you'll ever have.

It's moistened up with sugar and wine.
    Girls rub it between their legs
    and give it to the one they love.
  It's very powerful stuff.
It's baked in an oven at a hundred degrees.

Auntie's Snaps

She used to wag her finger, pulling out
the dusty box. And it wasn't the normal stuff –
family holidays, Christmases and such –

but men's pricks. She'd beckon me
closer, patting the couch beside her,
then spreading the album between us

started to flick, muttering a comment
as each page of penis polaroids
flopped open on our laps.

Now look at this my scallywag –
look how long and thin it is,
like a car's oil-dipper

and soft as a lady's ballroom slipper.
Would you give it a kiss?
Would you fatten it up with a lick to the tip?

Have you heard about the dainty fine tale
from the old French poet
about the serving of ham and rolls

and the bouncy serving girl
who rubbed her little flower clitoris
and went riding on a set of jumping balls?

Here – clasp your pretty peepers on this one,
it can't be much less
than a good ten inches long,

maybe more, perhaps,
from tip to base
and a gorgeous ginger thatch to rest upon.

Look – none has compared to this one
since that lengthy andouille sausage
from the seller man at the fair

and thirty sheets of blousy napkin
to mop off your hands and face!
Spiced with punchy herbs and thick as an arm!

Carnival from Davies' Window

They came in one by one,
a tiger-faced child with a currant bun,
a man with a tray of Mantuan nougat,

silky balls of bread and chocolate
filled with cream and cherries,
angel lilies, a kiss that's second to none.

They came in two by two,
the hippopotamus and the kangaroo;
with long spears of sticky nougat

and tinkling golden tambourines.
There was a man dressed as Venus
with a velvety penis as long as your arm.

They came in three by three –
great heaps of papier-mâché
formed in the shape of an ass.

The fox is wearing a paper hat
and he's chasing the red-haired woman
across Desire Street and into his den.

They came in four by four –
some by the window, some by the door.
Some did somersaults and cartwheels.

Some were dressed as astronauts
and took baths in the green fountain
with the little pissing boy Cupid.

They came in five by five,
some for the hills, some from the hive.
The wind got so high and mighty

it blew off someone's nightie
and tossed it six miles down the road
where Big Chief was sewing on sequins.

They came in six by six,
the little monkey up to his tricks.
Cool lemonade in the roaring afternoon

while the fire ants and the raccoon
sniff around your legs.
Take up that vine and use it as a flute.

The Hare

(after Alexander Carmichael)

Do nothing if thou doubt
My virtuosity and daring
My excellent skills
    At boxing and collecting.

I would never eat grass
But loved the sweet herbs
You could find on Tallack's hills
    And the place by the byre.

My fur like a bright fire
Was eyed by the women,
My long legs and flesh
    Were the things of the men.

It is a sad tale to tell
That my fun is now done
And the sport that I had
    Is stopped in its tracks.

They've taken my coat,
It is ripped from my back
And roasted my flesh
    On a red-roaring fire.

The celebrations of Spring
Seem a lifetime away
When I gave my full thrust
    To the things in my path.

Who could have thought
That a man would come down
With a snare and a bag
    Just to have me?

The celebrations of Spring
Seem a lifetime away,
When I boxed on the hills
   With my ancestors all.

We plucked off the herbs
Whenever we fancied
Though I fell into this snare
   Which was grievous for me.

Cute Little Rooster

Little rooster, me amigo! Now wait!
    You'll be the talk of the town.
        Put these sharp trousers on –
        they're best in the store!
    We won't skimp a dime.
Try on this dandy double-breasted coat.

They'll ask you where you got your style?
    Try out this fancy scarf –
        the tailor's cut it neat
        and nipped, a perfect fit
    and dapper. Put these trousers on –
all best in the store. We didn't skimp.

Little rooster – take your place at the table –
    right at the head if you like!
        Take the lion's share – green
        beans and stew, creamed
    corn, rum cake,
sticky squash pie, this soup by the ladle.

Little rooster – help us with our sums –
    help the bankers out.
        The commercial district's
        in a meltdown, a panic! –
    help them through it all.
Use your brains and mathematical mind!

Help the lawyers get through their days –
    all their intricate subtleties
        and tricks of the trade.
        Help them sort the cases
    and all the finicky books
till they're just right! Help them make a buck.

Little rooster – help the shopkeepers out
    then peel off your gloves.
        Take off your hat
        and give me that rat-a-tat-tat –
    set the bed frame rocking.
Let that thing between my sweet legs sing!

Little rooster – let me have your throat,
    I'll drive my teeth right in!
        Let me have your breast
        and press in these best
    of the best silver pins.
Let the blood flow! I'll hold your coat.

Wolf Called to Bird

I feel hot – do you feel hot? I'm thinking
      a shower – damn! it's hot. Icky.
What the devil's got into me?
Maybe take a step into a chest-
freezer, cool me down a little –
hold down that lid, just you be a dear.

Those angel blooms sure do look nice up there
      hanging off that big tree.
How about I pick you a posy?
Women like that sort of thing.
Damn! Why can't I get cool?
There's a river running down past my neck here.

If I was your boyfriend I'd take care of you;
      wouldn't treat you bad at all.
I'd love to take care of you (rubbing
his crotch). You look so good
(licking his lips). I'd make sure
you got (drooling) spoiled. Keep you safe.

Damn it! What are you looking at up there
      furry-face? I bet you can see
all the way to Grand Isle;
a couple of old codgers
leafing through some cookbook.
Just you get down here and give me a good time.

Horses Sally or Ivy Blue

So come on Lady – how do you like it?
    What are the women saying?
        How do I do it just right?
      Well – keep the pressure on
    but not too *too* much –
like something's squatting between there.

Like something's nosing past the folds of a –
    well, a lady's dress –
        a really big heavy rich one,
        you know, heavy as hell
    and rich as a rose.
Do you get me? Or nudging past silk.

And what about the tongue? O sweet one
    that's the easy part.
        Couple it up with little sucks –
        and not too much attack –
    like you're chasing a lone pea
inside a – jug of – milk – with your tongue!

Do you want me to stick a finger in?
    Is that what you want?
        If that's what you really fancy
        then two or three are dandy.
    And just like the mouth.
Just like you're kissing me on the mouth.

Someone might like it seven inches in
    and another light as a pin.
        But nothing too paddle-like,
        or like some great woofer
    sucking marrow out a bone.
Come on. Get to work you son-of-a-whore.

Appetite

The great tarts of her feet –
glossy black ponds,
berries big as fists, black
as the core of the night, and wet!

Dinner at Irene's Bistro

As you shucked the last oysters
onto your side plate
and ordered a lemon ice

I found myself in the guise of a large beetle
down amongst the spilt salt grains
and your slim-line after-dinner cigarettes.

I was a swarm of fifty thousand bees
floating up towards the Venus de Milo
and the damp patches on the ceiling.

I propped up the cold-cuts table
with my enormous body
as a massive brown bear

setting my teeth into the table legs,
my nails almost torn out
by the shaggy carpet.

I found myself as a booming moose,
antlers snagged in the chandelier
and my eyes runny from grill-smoke.

I was a great white and black bird
wheeling around your head
then alighting on the edge

of a soup-ladle
to roll out my plumage
with my beak in a bottle of Big Sticky.

I was a large hare with my fur on end
and prodigiously louping
over orange-bombes and pink brandies,

the dreaming bread and the searing pan,
a rope of cherries and the garlic,
into your lap.

Hot Illogical Dream in the Oiseau Hotel

Cutiepie   spread'em   *written on air or running water*
secretnoise   king dong   like a wagon
stormcloud   travellingfreakshow   *cork at sea*
electric oscillating fan   field of slips
fringe   dirtysummer   *unable to conceive of any other place*
negligee   Brett St.   Edwardian
sac-o-love   prettypleasing   blotcher   flasher
a mound of white roses   *a body as weightless*
as a strip of cane   gentle art of cupcaking   neatlyavoiding
whoa there   queen of the wheat   porch
by stages   shadowboxing   *just by the sound of it*
goosedown   half-sleep   heavy ankles   pianoforte
camomile   figs   stairs   toupee and moustache
no clothes at all underneath   *what was he thinking?*
Adam's apple   blindfold   feet   patch   pipe
thicket   float   bird   *drawn out at the root*
biscuit-coloured hair   spit   *even in the water they'd sway*
just cooling

The Duel

(after the Gond)

My face is full of sin
His mouth is an axle turn
My lips are a spanner in the works
His fingertips are a cocker spaniel
My palms are white as snow
His teeth are lovely as marble
My eyelids are wild as a Turkish dervish dance
His back is blond as a stone
My mouth is yellow as cornmeal
His mouth is beautiful as a river
He is the flint,
But he has not got the better of me,
His flint has become the touchstone of my soul.

And How Those Riders Go!

And
they rode
through the Far Field,
the Mean Field, the Field of Eyes,
the Disused Field, the Barn Field,
the Yield Field, the Wizened Field,
the Field of the Silver Slipper,
the Warren Field, the Gypsy Field,
the Old Field, the Green Field,
the Hide and Seek Field,
the Top Hat Field, the Rice Field,
the 'Nice Thing' Field, the Fruit Store Field,
the Velvet-green Wood Field, the *O-la* Field,
the Box Room Field,
the Face Like a Plate of Cowflop Field,
the Devil-may-care Field,
the Odd Field
and
they rode
through the Far Field too.

Hair and My Grandmother's Ring

O Mother used to cut it with a knife
     taken from the butcher's bag
or the hatchet from the stairs.
I'd sit in the chair
and let her cut it back;
I suck from a dish of green-tops and beef.

My old grandmother's plaited my hair,
     thin as a sapling.
She'd smear some Glory on
with the flat of her ancient palm
and turn her wedding ring
three times for luck and sometimes four.

Really Drunk in Matassa's Bar

(after Meleager)

Sweetness, I'll give you something to tell her –
and straight from the hip.
Tell her she's a two-faced –

no, no – let's have that rephrased –
a useless Quasimodo-like –
wait a minute the words are on my tongue.

Tell her she's fifth or sixth on my list of fucks
and that's pretty low.
Say she's second to an encounter

with an absolute horror
picked up one night
while smashed on cocaine and strong drinks.

In fact Sweetness, tell her I'm doing fine.
Tell her my boats are home
and they're stuffed to the gunnels

with all manner of luxury goods
and I'm feathering my nest.
Tell her I'm up and doing the rounds again.

Tell her I'm set up with a new woman –
a honey-dipped blessing.
Tell her you can't sleep some nights

with all the noisy fuck-fucking
till four in the morning.
Tell her I'm so tired I walk about in a dream.

Tell her I've had my hair all cut
and it suits my face.
It looks like it's the real thing.

Tell her I've got a new wardrobe
and no one's surprised.
Tell her I've matched it all with pricy boots.

Tell her I've shed off those extra pounds;
or, in fact – no, no –
tell her I've put a whole load on.

Tell her I'm always dining out
and you've heard stories
I'm rolling in at dawn and I'm laughing.

In Room 42 of Hotel Oiseau, Under the Covers!

O she spreads all right:
a flamingo's stubby fantail
dancing in the night!

Supper Dish

I've been up since crack of dawn,
it's taken all day –
the stock's getting thicker now,
it's climbing up the pan.
Two big marrowbones,
chosen specially for you;
these beans are top-rate choice,
mixed in a little ham.

Here's a dish of daddy crawfish,
smeared with red sauce,
suck these right up,
they're good and'll make you strong.
What really could be better, baby,
that's it my little baby,
you just suck so very hard,
take the enamel off this spoon.

Curse Poems

I

O silent queen of the long afternoon,
 the silver slice, the pretty cake,
  the tinkling china teacups.
  Where'd you get those liver spots
 and those hairs above your lip?
Whoever thought you'd get so old so soon?

That's not some jive record you're hearing.
 They're carving out your coffin
  from a load of dirty boards
  found on Pontchartrain's shores.
 They've laid them on the lawn;
the nails are picked, the fast saw's moving.

II

That big old bed was simply on fire!
 Those colossi went to task!
  They crawled from the seams
  or parachuted right in
 like crazy daredevils!
A feast's to be had and that's for sure.

You couldn't say for sure if it was man,
 or beast or what,
  the way it jumped and ran,
  twisted and turned –
 screaming out to please Stop!
Red raw and weeping – stripped to the bone.

III

Fresh as the first rose of the old world,
   the tip bright as a nipple –
      the new bloom; thrust
      between the old red crust
    that now lies thick with ferns
and palms and a bright rose standing proud.

Standing there in a daze of white light
   the day's getting hotter.
      There's a dance of fresh dews
      lifting off the fine few
    petals at the nub; the scent's
singular and lovely; foreboding something.

The first line of this poem is kick-started by W.S. Graham's
'O Gentle Queen of the Afternoon'.

The Dog: A Tale of Love, Bad Love and Longing

1

Then devilish, rooting for pearls –
her trousers, gusset, blouse –
her cuffs – a scent – cunty! –
rises up through the lot.
She's been seeing Major Cott
on Fridays and Sundays
for seven months straight now.
A dirty, blousy, wayward girl.

2

I plough down, upend, career –
a cold and scentless thing,
like glass –
geegaws, a diamond ring –
things she'd snaffle and stash
from her ugly old man.
She'd gladly live in a caravan
a million miles from here.

3

An endless line of snout –
I'll sing to you and push
my body through the seven
zones of palpable pleasure:
toadstools, minerals,
mossy turds,
sweet-peas, semen and blood.
I'll root and rout them out.

4

Of course there're tales to tell –
these back up pell-mell.
A cleaver crashes skulls –
well, one time, yes.
The woods a hush-hush place
as that grave was dug
and the body flopped in.
The wallet went straight down the well.

5

By nine the window's up
and a big bun's cooling.
Sign: Ready when you are.
The Kansas man cleans up,
shifts a rag and cup.
He sorts his hair in the mirror.
Sign: Ready and waiting.
He clutches his bag and comes.

6

Her hair, well what's to say?
That's white gold spun
through the fingers of Homunculi.
It's sweeties, herbs –
saffron, maybe – it's weeds.
Sometimes peppery,
throwaway candies, a plum
on a dish in the sun.

7

The skin, well that's a tale:
a fairy tale, all that –
corn and spice and sugar.
(A fairy makes nice things
with pretty things inside.)
They bet to find its peer
in the woods-floor hut
but they're drunk, and fail.

Couplet

Dirty muck, instead of king and queen
I'll replace you now with pea and bean.

A Kiss as a Dish

Salt, of course,
little by little, tasting as you go.

Fruits of the Forest!

and took a pot of custard to grandma...

Cut the fig like a ham –
thin-thin and lengthways,
nestle it on my tongue.
A light year, a won-
der-ful-ex-per-i-ence!
As light as my slipper in dung!
(if I were a little princess,
smarmy-mouthed, and I am!)

Lady Voodoo Talks for a Bit

Voodoo, the most charming one on earth
lays out dolly's legs and arms
gently, gently like she was a spider

with a sack of silky eggs inside her.
She combs out dolly's long black hair
and lifts her skirt right up past her neck.

(Little dolly, Voodoo's taken you up now
and plans to rub-rub fire
deep deep inside your veins,

she plans to coat your lengthy hair
with yellow dust and food.
She'll slide on into her blazing girdle of fire

and roll roll her hands, just so, just to and fro,
like an Ibo tribesman
trying to start his evening fire

for a snake, a mouse and a hare.
I'll take up my ashy stick
and my green bottle of dark Africa;

I'll take up my petal and my yellow shell
till you're smooth as a lozenge.
I'll give you the crush of my petaly soup

and my pig brains in slop.
Let me comb out your long black hair
and fix on a little lipstick from my stash.

Let's take our place now by the old graveside
and look over our treats:
candies, false teeth, condoms,

a wig, a cross, cigarettes,
a bottle of gin, driftwood
all laid out neat by the side of the grave.)

The Dreamers and Boy Rabbit

There was only the murmur of the night, the gin.
　　I'll tell you how it fell.
　　　　And the loud tock tock
　　　　of the hallway clock
　　that gave us all the creeps.
It brought out the bad smell of the curtains.

After the song the villagers killed boy rabbit.
　　It turned out this way:
　　　　they cut his body in chunks,
　　　　festooned his lengthy intestines
　　with a load of baubles and bells
around the walkways, down by Candy Market.

They cut him into bite-sized bobs of meat,
　　diced and well peppered.
　　　　They threw him in a pot
　　　　with stock and a carrot
　　to serve for a lunch.
They rolled his sweetbreads in salt and beet.

His spirit hovered higher than the moon –
　　like Baron Munchausen's bees.
　　　　They'd tried to pull it down
　　　　with a slotted spoon
　　and silver tinkling cups.
They opened up a velvet box and forced it in.

The rabbit danced a dance with Mr Teat.
　　His wife was a terrible whore.
　　　　One little glass of champagne
　　　　she'd be legless again
　　with her great fat arms
around some random stranger on the street.

Move a muscle and they'll break your neck.
  They chopped up the rabbit.
      They guzzled buckets of champagne;
      the whore got drunk again
  and so did Mr Teat.
And only the murmur of the gin, the night.

Eulalie

No matter what others have whispered
you're the ugliest bitch
who ever walked these streets.

Let me tell you how it is
and I'll shoot from the hip –
the most bloated, ugly, horse-faced bastard.

You've certainly a 'lived-in-ness' to you –
had a few late nights?
Your hair's like a filthy mop

and your arse is a chop –
not a lean cut –
no, no. More like a chew-toy for mutts.

Here's a surprise. Eulalie's taken her shoes
and moseyed on down
to the Ring-a-Ding-Ding

to claim the latest fashion
then grab herself a man.
Ha! Her singing and dancing acts – hideous.

Quiet everyone – Eulalie's having a dream!
There's a big dark suitor
who's brought her scarlet blooms

and they're very, very nice.
Wake up Eulalie – it's fake!
Hey Eulalie – you've a face like a ham.

Open up that dirty mouth of yours –
I know what we'll see:
a dirty writhing gooey mess.

What's it like so far away up there?
You're just too busy being tall.
It must be such a horrible fix

having legs like toothpicks
and always craning your neck.
And the wind-speeds that tousle your hair.

Travelling Eye (Looking Down Summer)

Past St Peter's and Desire Street, past
the red love heart shaped hibiscus
and Uncle Earl in his cast

sipping a cup of coffee, past
the hanging gardens,
then turning left, past the *Gasthouse*.

Past old Nellie knitting a sock, past
the red phone booth
burning in the sun

(that's been kaput now
for almost three weeks) past
the melons; you're nearly there, nearly there.

Past the little restaurant on the corner,
owned by the Frenchman,
and where they'll be cooking up

pumpkins and raisins,
coriander and cinnamon
and plums and ginger to stuff in pastries.

Over the high walls into the secret garden
off Ursuline Street,
where my friend and me

shattered our soft knees
trying to net fruit,
or catch lovely ladies bathing in the nude!

Past all those wooden shutters – green
and yellow and blue
shut close-tight

in the middle of the day
and all whilst the sun is blazing!
What the devil is going on behind there? –

Homoerotic love affairs, horrible marital
breakdowns, arguments
and lots of monkey business!

Well that's our guess,
and this little place
stinks of horse shit all the year round.

Past the house where they brew damson gin
in long classy thin
lovely bottles, past

the Man with the Glass Eyes
and his big polished trombone;
ah you're nearly there; it's almost in your reach.

Up at Betsy Twelves'

And nor was I visited by sickness, a dream
    of the clammy homunculus –
        pug-ugly, pigeon-chested;
        bad breath and brittle-boned –
    the horrible dwarf from hell,
firing up his shambolic red love boat

for a trip around the dark, craggy islands –
    a lunch of canapés and lobsters;
        fish stew; bisque
        and slimy syllabub;
    the pouch of fumy love letters
he'd been sending all summer, mercilessly...

Things You Didn't Know, But You Did

Of course she knew a trick or two,
things she'd learned from her mother
or her time in a boat at sea,

but I also knew a few tricks
and wasn't slow at all
in sizing up my opponent.

We stood close together
till my legs went from under me
as if she'd turned out a blanket.

I managed to slide some fingers
past her lips
and yank her tongue like a bell-rope.

Any blows to my head and neck
I fended off with my palms
and some very good footwork.

I was dripping with sweat
but I shoved my hands deep in her pockets
and drove my fists into her buttocks

while red and black specks
swam in front of my eyes
from the sheer pressure of her hold,

her arm tight across my chest
sending my shoulders so far back
I thought they'd touch the ground

till we both fell down
face to face in the dust,
a slight breeze working over us.